MW01130782

Moray Eels

by Lindsay Shaffer

BLASTOFF!
2
READERS

BELLWETHER MEDIA • MINNEAPOLIS, MN

Note to Librarians, Teachers, and Parents:

Blastoff! Readers are carefully developed by literacy experts and combine standards-based content with developmentally appropriate text.

Level 1 provides the most support through repetition of high-frequency words, light text, predictable sentence patterns, and strong visual support.

Level 2 offers early readers a bit more challenge through varied simple sentences, increased text load, and less repetition of high-frequency words.

Level 3 advances early-fluent readers toward fluency through increased text and concept load, less reliance on visuals, longer sentences, and more literary language.

Level 4 builds reading stamina by providing more text per page, increased use of punctuation, greater variation in sentence patterns, and increasingly challenging vocabulary.

Level 5 encourages children to move from "learning to read" to "reading to learn" by providing even more text, varied writing styles, and less familiar topics.

Whichever book is right for your reader, Blastoff! Readers are the perfect books to build confidence and encourage a love of reading that will last a lifetime!

This edition first published in 2020 by Bellwether Media, Inc.

No part of this publication may be reproduced in whole or in part without written permission of the publisher. For information regarding permission, write to Bellwether Media, Inc., Attention: Permissions Department, 6012 Blue Circle Drive, Minnetonka, MN 55343.

Library of Congress Cataloging-in-Publication Data

Names: Shaffer, Lindsay, author.
Title: Moray Eels / by Lindsay Shaffer.
Description: Minneapolis, MN : Bellwether Media, Inc., 2020. |
  Series: Animals of the coral reef | Includes bibliographical references and index. | Audience: Ages 5-8 |
  Audience: Grades K-1 | Summary: "Relevant images match informative text in this introduction to moray eels.
  Intended for students in kindergarten through third grade"-- Provided by publisher.
Identifiers: LCCN 2019033072 (print) | LCCN 2019033073 (ebook) | ISBN 9781644871324 (library binding) |
ISBN 9781618918147 (ebook)
Subjects: LCSH: Morays--Juvenile literature.
Classification: LCC QL638.M875 S53 2020 (print) | LCC QL638.M875 (ebook) | DDC 597/.43--dc23
LC record available at https://lccn.loc.gov/2019033072
LC ebook record available at https://lccn.loc.gov/2019033073

Text copyright © 2020 by Bellwether Media, Inc. BLASTOFF! READERS and associated logos are trademarks and/or registered trademarks of Bellwether Media, Inc.

Editor: Betsy Rathburn   Designer: Laura Sowers

Printed in the United States of America, North Mankato, MN.

Table of Contents

Life in the Coral Reef

giant moray eel

Moray eels live in warm ocean waters around the world.

Many make homes in
the coral reef **biome**.

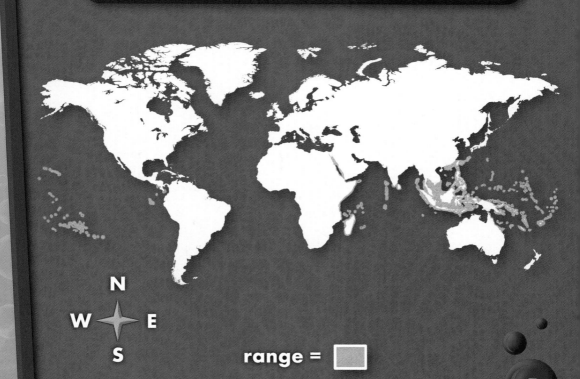

Giant Moray Eel Range

N

W ✦ E

S

range = ☐

5

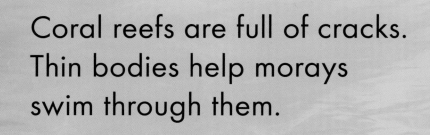

Coral reefs are full of cracks.
Thin bodies help morays
swim through them.

yellow-edged moray eel

Mucus protects morays' skin from sharp **corals**.

Some morays are brightly colored. Many have spots or stripes.

dragon moray eel

Special Adaptations

mucus on skin

sharp teeth

long, thin body

These give them **camouflage** in the colorful coral reef!

Coral reefs are full of **predators**. Morays hide to stay safe.

They swim backwards
into hiding places!

green moray eel

Moray eels often have **parasites**. They visit **cleaning stations** to stay healthy.

Shrimp and fish eat parasites off the eels' skin!

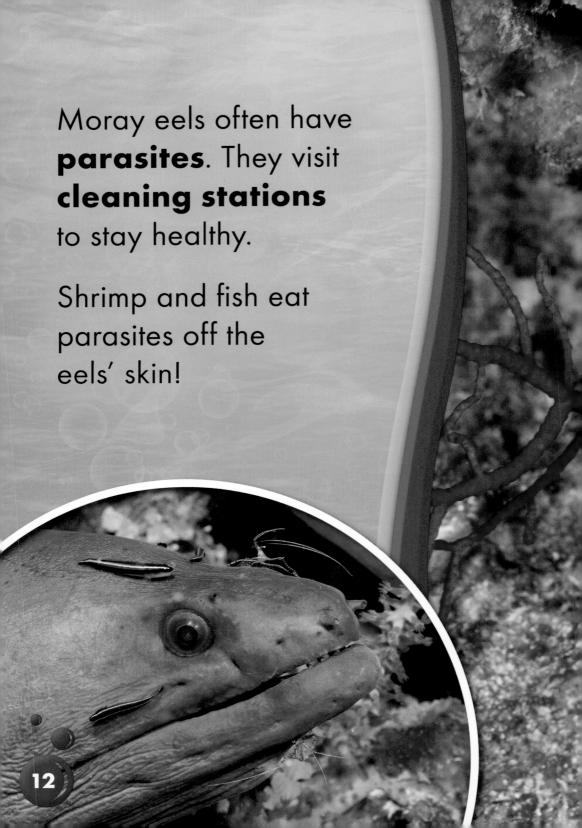

Giant Moray Eel Stats

Least Concern	Near Threatened	Vulnerable	Endangered	Critically Endangered	Extinct in the Wild	Extinct

conservation status: least concern

life span: up to 30 years

Sharp Teeth and Teamwork

Most morays hunt at night. Strong senses help them find **prey**.

They sniff out tasty fishes and **mollusks**!

These **carnivores** have
two sets of sharp teeth.

One set is inside their throats. It springs forward to grab prey!

Some morays team up
with other fish to hunt.

Moray Eel Diet

Caribbean reef octopuses

flamboyant cuttlefish

gall crabs

The fish lead morays to hidden food. Morays slip into the cracks for a meal!

Some morays tie themselves in knots around prey. This squeezes meals into smaller bites.

leopard moray eel

These tough fishes find plenty to eat in the coral reef biome!

Glossary

biome—a large area with certain plants, animals, and weather

camouflage—the ability to blend in with the surroundings

carnivores—animals that only eat meat

cleaning stations—places in the ocean where fish are cleaned by shrimps and cleaner fish

corals—the living ocean animals that build coral reefs

mollusks—animals with no backbones such as snails, octopuses, and squids; mollusks usually have hard shells.

mucus—a clear liquid that covers the body of a moray eel

parasites—creatures that live on other living things and use them for food; parasites harm their hosts.

predators—animals that hunt other animals for food

prey—animals that are hunted by other animals for food

To Learn More

AT THE LIBRARY

Beaton, Kathryn. *Discover Moray Eels.* Ann Arbor, Mich.: Cherry Lake Publishing, 2016.

Hulick, Kathryn. *Coral Reefs.* New York, N.Y.: AV2 by Weigl, 2019.

Morlock, Theresa. *Electric Eels.* New York, N.Y.: Gareth Stevens Publishing, 2017.

ON THE WEB

FACTSURFER

Factsurfer.com gives you a safe, fun way to find more information.

1. Go to www.factsurfer.com.

2. Enter "moray eels" into the search box and click Q.

3. Select your book cover to see a list of related web sites.

Index

The images in this book are reproduced through the courtesy of: Evlakhov Valeriy, front cover (eel); John_Walker, front cover (coral), pp. 2-3; Rich Carey, pp. 4-5; Magnus Larsson, pp. 6-7; Luis Miguel Casado Gracia, p. 7; Ara Yamamoto, p. 8; Kichigin, p. 9 (left); SergeUWPhoto, p. 9 (right); Placebo365, p. 10; Wet Lizard Photography, pp. 10-11; Joe Belanger, p. 12; cbimages/ Alamy, pp. 12-13; sergemi, p. 14; Hyoungho Lee, pp. 14-15; fenkieandreas, pp. 16-17; Ellen Hu, p. 17; Nature Picture Library/ Alamy, p. 18; John A. Anderson, p. 19 (Caribbean reef octopuses); Mike Workman, p. 19 (flamboyant cuttlefish); Oksana Maksymova, p. 19 (gall crabs); Andrea Izzotti, pp. 20-21; Aaronejbull87, p. 21; Leonardo Gonzalez, p. 22.